# Dressing Skeletons

D1714492

## ALSO BY MARIA R. PALACIOS

The Female King (poetry)

Karate on Wheels: A Journey of Self Discovery

Criptionary: Disability Humor & Satire

The Goddess in This Woman:
A Journal for the Woman's Soul

The Girl in This Goddess:
An Empowerment Journal
for Girls and Young Women

The Big Little Black Book: An Address Book
Revealing What Women Want Men to Know

# Dressing Skeletons

## A Poetic Tribute To Frida Kahlo

*Maria R. Palacios*

Atahualpa Press, Houston, TX

DRESSING SKELETONS:
A Poetic Tribute to Frida Kahlo
Copyright © 2015 by Maria R. Palacios
www.facebook.com/writerpoetgoddessonwheels

Cover Art Copyright © 2007 by Sabrina Zarco
www.SabrinaZarco.com

Library of Congress Control Number:
2015909893

FIRST EDITION

ISBN: 978-0972648387

Printed in the United States of America

Cover Graphic Design by Laura Fiscal

Editing and Interior Design by
WeaselWorks Freelance Editing
www.facebook.com/WeaselWorks

Published by Atahualpa Press
Houston, Texas 77072

*For Frida Kahlo, and for all those who
love the immortality of her art.*

"I understand your demons, your monsters – the ones that make you paint feet, the ones that make me write about shoes.

"You see... I have dressed a few skeletons of my own. Mine wear boots and bracelets and lingerie, and strip themselves into poems the way yours do into colors – the colors of death, although you may be painting life."

> — Maria R. Palacios, from the eponymous entry of this collection

Hear a passionate, live performance of this title by the author herself at this internet address:

https://www.youtube.com/watch?v=xDMsuVLozxE

# TABLE OF CONTENTS

# Dressing Skeletons

## *Addiction*

In reality,

I am an addict –

an addict

of your poison and your pain.

You are my droughts

and my heavy rains,

the water I drink

and the ink

of my pen.

Yes,

I am addicted to you –

addicted

to every crevice

and every crack,

every pore

of your art,

the flesh of your name,

things that stay the same

over time.


I'm addicted to you –

to your fruits

and your plates,

addicted to your sadness.

The same monsters that made you paint

make me write.

They grab me

and cleave me

and leave me to die.


That's why I drink you slowly,

sipping your bitter sorrows

and the ripeness of your colors;

a teaspoon of honey

and some limes.

I let you melt

between my lines

then rift and drift

apart.

But I come back,

wanting more of you,

more of us,

more of your moons

and your suns,

more of your darkness –

more of this consuming rush.

We are each other's love affair,

each other's past,

each other's addiction

and vice,

and yet

above it all,

we rise.

We rise like a cloud of smoke.

We rise

like the morning fog,

like Lazarus after the third day,

like Jesus after the third fall.

Despite anything,

we rise,

and will continue to rise

until the fix wears off.

## Cocktail of Memories

I have a few *Diegos*

in my past,

men whose names still hurt

between my lips

and whose memory burns

between my breasts;

men who left me to bleed

after my heart was torn

and who, despite all this,

I still love.

The *Diegos* of my past

came early in my youth,

when sixteen and forty-five were lovers

lost under the covers

of sin.

My first *Diego*

was a forbidden man.

My first sin of sixteen

was a mortal one,

an intense affair,

another woman's worst nightmare;

that's who I became

at sixteen.


Yes,

at sixteen

I was already you,

wearing your turquoise and your blue,

your affairs and your sorrows.

I lived your tomorrows

and painted the sadness

of your happy colors

in my words.


You drink the ink

of my poems.

I drink the poison of your pain,

mix your name in a martini

and get lost in the past,

get lost in you,

lost in the seams of your dress

where I kiss

and I bless

your

wounds.

## *Frida without the Sadness*

*Frida! Frida! Frida!*

Why does your pain feel so real?

Why do your scars

reside on my flesh?

Your wounds always so fresh,

your love always so raw

and so...

intense.


Every polio year that goes by

I seem to know more of you,

the how and why

of your Woman Muse,

the love affairs that fuse

the soul.

The skeletons we dress in red

and white

become the hungry wolves we are,

lonesome lovers

in a moonless night in May.

Ironically,

May was probably kinder to you.

It was July

that gave you life

and brought you death,

July that came and went

like the summer breeze

it always is.


And we both know

about lonesome nights

and endless loves,

the kind that mark us for life

like the scar we wear

on our backs.

In every stitch

we rip ourselves apart

in the name

of love.

Maybe that's why

you painted skulls,

memories

emptied

into the eyes of a man

after making love.

I paint words, one by one,

the same way

you painted bones

(paper dresses

for the paper dolls we become,

marching in our own revolution).

We don't claim to save the world,

but we try

to save ourselves

through our art.

"Frida without the sadness,"

some may say,

maybe without knowing

there is no such thing,

like there is no such thing as my feet

learning to dance.

You and I live forever in a trance

of immense sadness

and immense love.

Many dress like you,

wearing your happy colors,

your jewelry and your brow,

but do they understand

how it really is

to be you,

like I do?


The *Diegos* that made us bleed,

the lovers

that helped us breathe,

only to let us die

again.

And do they really understand

our pain?

Years of hospital beds

empty of love.

Years of doodling

with pencils and markers,

writing love notes

on the body cast that imprisoned us.

Years of people in white,

shooting morphine and lies

into our veins.

How many have loved

like us?

Lovers stretched across the map...

clotheslines where our dresses hang,

from New York

to San Francisco,

your *Casa Azul* dressed in green

as if you'd come back

through me

a little happier this time.

Perhaps I really am

this twisted version of you,

another genre of Frida,

with your matter-of-fact approach

to sex,

your intense approach to love.

I have been you for so long

that you have settled

into my words –

my words of pain,

my words of hope,

my words

of eternal hunger.

The same

that made you paint death,

the same

that makes me write life,

the self-portraits you left

and the one

I now paint

of us

through this poem.

## Fruit of Life

Your *Fruits of the Earth* ripen

in my poems.

They fall off the tree.

"Bite me," they beg,

and when I do,

they bleed

on my page.


Your paintings sprout words.

They grow limbs and toes,

cactus and melons,

and twisted metaphors.


Your fruits of the earth ripen.

"Eat me," they plead.

I can't refuse.

I can go days without food,

feasting only on your colors.

I confess my sins on paper

on an empty stomach.

No rice or beans;

only painted fruit will do.


Your reality

blends with my moon.

We devour each other like wolves.

I enter

your forbidden zones,

the contour of bones

that insist on living

long after

they have turned

to dust.

## Holding On

I have met her before

and could have gone with her

at any given chance,

any

of the thirty-some times

I went under the knife.

I could have gone with her,

but I always chose

to hold on

to life.

Death has always haunted me.

She calls me to her side.

She keeps my legs cold at night

and brings me close

to your name.


My words

rise like bread

when you enter my thoughts,

so I add holy water to your memory.

I take my Catholic upbringing –

crucifix above the bed,

rosary beads and Hail Marys,

the silence

of cemeteries,

guilt –

at its best.

You know the rest

is history:

the love affairs we keep hidden.

the most delicious fruit

is the forbidden.

*That*

is the taste of sin.


And you and I know sin

with the same intimacy we know death.

We could have gone with her

at any given chance

but while you chose to let go,

I still choose to hold on

to life.

## Dressing Skeletons

You paint

the canvas of my mind.

You paint skeletons and dresses,

big earrings

and death roses.


You paint hair, teeth and bones –

the things that never really die,

the things

maggots can't digest.

I hang your dresses, your paintings,

your unwritten poems,

the bleeding hearts of melons,

the sad faces of coconuts.

I hang your *Still Life*,

your *Naturaleza Muerta,*

and your scars

along with mine.


I understand your demons,

your monsters –

the ones that make you paint feet,

the ones that make me write

about shoes.

You see...

I have dressed

a few skeletons of my own.

Mine wear boots and bracelets

and lingerie,

and strip themselves into poems

the way yours do into colors –

the colors of death,

although

you may be painting

life.


And so,

I hang your dresses and your thorns,

your internal organs,

the umbilical cord of your art,

the souls

of the bones we cover,

your moon,

your monkeys and your sun.


I hang all your things

next to mine,

next to the man I love,

the men I've loved,

and the women

I have dreamed of loving.


Like you, I know love.

I know it in its crudest form.

I know its third eye,

its cannibalistic tendencies,

the way it devours us,

leaving

no remains to bury,

no ashes to scatter,

no tombstone

where to engrave

memories.


I wear your painted dresses.

You wear

my metaphors.


Bones rattle and shiver.

We're feeling cold,

but the dead stay cold,

even

after we've been

dressed.

## I Am You

I find you

wherever I happen to be.

You live in my jewelry box

and in my closet.

You live

in all the shoes I'll never wear

and all the songs I'll never dance.

You live in the scar on my back

and in the love of signatures

left

on a body cast.


You live

in waiting rooms and hospital beds,

on the hard surface

of operating tables.

In the coldness of steel,

the turning of wheels,

and bus rides to nowhere, you live.


You live, and I find you,

wherever I happen to be,

because we know

what the dead think.

We know their poems,

their color;

the decomposition of words

and the loudness of silence, we know.


And so, you live in me

and I live

in you.

We are

each other's tombstones,

each other's color.

My words scream

the colors of you:

your yellows and your browns,

the earthiness of you;

the reds that bleed on the page,

the broken spine of dreams;

the orange that makes you paint

the wombs of papayas

and the intestines of love,

because love itself is a body –

one that bleeds

through your art.


And your art speaks my language:

*me habla de tus tristezas*

(it talks about your sadness).

It talks about the two of you...

the *Two Fridas* you painted,

the double life

all women live,

and how we always

split ourselves in half.


That's why my words

scream your name

and find you

in the skin of melons

and the fruit I cut into poems,

the way you cut yours into paintings.


You breathe in color

and exhale poems –

the poems you become

through my words.

I know what it's like to be you.

Not many people do, but I do.  I do.

I know, like you,

how love inhales you

and smokes you away slowly,

like a burning cigarette.

Oh, God!

I also know

the pleasure of a cigarette

and the heat of tequila,

the way it burns words in your throat,

makes you spit out fire,

turns you

into the dragon you become –

for love, for lust

for art.


Your thorns claw me,

and burn my skin

with images that become you

and poems that become me,

until you and I

can't tell who's who.

Our souls have merged.

You have painted my poems

again.


Words have grown

between my fingers

the way color grew

between yours,

and together we bleed

poems.

## Insomnia

I keep the dark poems

to myself,

let them soak in water

like beans,

let them puff up and swell,

scream and yell

in my pot of hot temper,

the spicy *Latina* side of me;

the Frida in my words,

my knives and my swords,

the poems that bite,

cut,

and make me bleed.


My dark poems have claws.

They cling

to the thread of my memories

and take me back to age nine

when I thought I could fight

six

of the people in white

hiding behind their masks

as my nails dug into their flesh.

My dark poems were fresh

beneath their skin.

I'm not exactly sure

what made me fight.

I guess I was afraid to fall asleep,

and afraid to wake up

to a scar unknown

when the final stitch was sewn,

and the last line stretched

across my page.


I watched the needle pushing in

as I tried to bite

the closest hand.

In the end

the needle won.

I woke up

to a scar unknown

and the people in white

above my bed.

Forty years have passed

since then.

I can still feel the flesh

beneath my words.

That's why I keep

the dark poems to myself.

I keep them on a leash

and keep them tame.

By now they have grown

sharper claws

and larger teeth.

They have become

panther and lioness,

but sometimes

they're still afraid

to fall asleep.

# *Laundry*

My dark side is gray

and cold.

Memories leak from the roof.

They fall like water.

The painful ones splatter

and make me write.

They're the ones I recite

between prayers.


I hold a crucifix

seeking redemption from madness –

the madness of love

and lust,

the madness of you

running though my past.


You make me give birth to words –

words that sprout thorns,

bits and pieces of you,

and painted toes.


Perhaps I understand you

a little too well...

our twisted love affairs

and our obsessions,

our secrets,

our guilt,

and our confessions

(even the ones never made) –

things that never fade away

no matter how hard we try.

Those stay with us

until we die,

and then some.

That's how you and I

become

one.


That's how we live

and reincarnate ourselves

into each other.

Your painted poems,

my written paintings

live together

like roommates

in different dimensions.


You possess my pen

and paint my words.

My dark side becomes you.

I sink in the coldness of your metaphors.

Your colors begin to foam like soap.


So I wash your dresses

in my prayers,

wash them by hand

with "Our Fathers" and "Hail Marys,"

like the women in small villages

who wash and pray

until their hands bleed.


I hang your dresses to dry,

each one

carefully pinned to a line.

Your colors become mine.

We become

women on a washing stone,

praying

and washing away

our sins

until all the guilt

is gone.

## Loneliness

I come to you like an addict,

desperate for a fix

of your fermented colors,

your tequila

and your mescal.

I've never eaten the worm,

but in the end,

the worm always eats

me.

I come to you

and paint myself nude

on your canvas.

I mourn your losses

and feel your pain.

I have become you again.

I always do

in my moments of darkness.


Loneliness has too many letters

to really say I feel

alone.

Sadness just has a way

of creeping into my senses.

It makes me spill words

on my blank pages.

I become as ageless

as you,

the blood of your red,

the tears of your blue;

I can't stop weeping

your poems.

## Memories

I woke up one day

and I was

you.

I was one of the Fridas

in your paintings.

I was the other you,

wearing your skirts and your wounds,

wearing your colors,

the skin of your art

against my metal braces,

the freedom

of untied shoelaces

flirting

with my immobile feet.


I woke up one day

and I was you,

wearing your scar on my back,

and my own memories

of the rack

stretching bones

into normality.


Like yours,

my years of polio were cold –

the cadaverous presence

of Death

holding my hand,

the kiss of morphine

burning my veins,

the people in white, surgical masks,

and the bleeding cactus

of your plates.


My years of polio were you,

my early poems,

tentative lines

where your dresses hung

along with my hospital gown,

white and blue patterns of forever,

and a clock

that had stopped attempting

to awaken hope behind the masks

of the people in white,

who stole seven

of my nine lives

and all nine of yours

one night.


Maybe that's why

I woke up as you.

I woke up cold like the polio years.

I became your written paintings,

words dressed in blood red

and black,

the indifference

of the people in white

and the smell of fear

in the air.

I have also been there.  Yes.

I have been there.


And like you,

I grew time

between the broken hands of a clock.

Tick-Tock.

I become you

again.


From beginning to end,

your nightmares

are my déjà vus,

the coldness

of operating rooms,

my Incan suns

and your Aztec moons.


I woke up one day

as you

and felt your sadness

running through my metaphors.

Your ocean

washed over my shores.

Your salt

painted my cheeks with tears.

Our monsters

have always been real.

That's why you paint.

That's why I write.

I take your broken heart.

Let it rest on the page

next to my words.

We get lost

within each other

like lovers.

Your colors blend with mine.

I watch you come back to life

and paint yourself

into my words.

# Miscarriage

There is a cemetery

where dreams are buried,

the stillbirth of some poems,

words that never learned to breathe

outside the page;

the stumps of sacred trees

and bloody sheets

are buried there.


There are no flowers,

there is no funeral –

just nameless tombs

and the kiss of Death

before limbs

had a chance

to grow.

## *Pain*

I wake up some mornings

and feel your past

calling me.

Neurons

threaten to commit suicide,

arms

that insist on living,

lungs

that get bored with air:

Inflate. ... Deflate.

You call my name

in the moon of October.


I surrender to you.

Your paintings speak my truths.

I write by instinct,

by the grip of my gut.

My superstitions become art

the way yours did

and do.

I don't know how to live

without you,

without your claws and your thorns

and achy bones

randomly thrown together

as a body.


I don't know how to say goodbye

or set you free.

How easy it is for you

to be me.

I know you wanted

to never return,

but when you did,

you chose another broken body

to live in.


Your pain

crawls slowly

up and down my spine.

Your monsters

become mine.

Some things stay the same.

I hold your name

in my hands

in the moon

of October.

## Naturaleza Muerta

I won't die young

like you.

I'm already old

in polio years.

I count years like a dog,

an extra set of seven

for each one that goes by,

plus all the broken mirrors

and broken promises

that supposedly bring

seven years of bad luck.

Seven times six is forty-two.

I'm always around the corner

from you.

How many full moons have there been in
my life?

By the time I'm done counting,

I'll no longer be young.


I won't die young

like you,

so my poems invent

another version of you,

one that hurts less

and laughs more,

one that lives long enough

to be old.


I don't have your *Casa Azul*.

My *Casa Azul* is green.

My colors are often

far away from blue.

Blue makes me cold.

Blue

makes me blue.


My colors are warm yellows

and reds,

black, green, and bright orange.

Like yours,

they are loud and mouthy.

They drink tequila

and they smoke,

but only

in my poems.


I feel

the immortality of you

crawling through my senses,

the ashes

of our most naked thoughts,

secrets

beneath a body cast,

the polio years,

and the cold legs.

The same monsters that haunted you

now live

under my bed.


By now they're tame.

I feed them scraps of poetry,

words that never make it

into the final draft,

the fatty ends of my creativity;

I feed them that.


I take each one of your colors

and bite

into your painted fruit,

into the heart of your pain

and your dreams,

the ones

you couldn't name,

the ones you couldn't kiss

goodbye.


Your art breathes in my poem.

The paper lungs

of your still life

inflate

with words.

You breathe again.

You live again.

You inhale me and absorb me

and make love to my page.

Death

does not frighten me.

We have always been

good friends.

## Self-Portrait

You wake up in my poems

and open your eyes

when I look into mine.


The same demons that possessed you,

possess me,

and I write

with your name dressed in red.

The ink of my pen

runs

through the veins of your art.

You had hoped

to never come back

but now you know

you never left.

You simply grew poems

between your hands

and kept on living.

Your tired fruits

rest on my page

and sleep in the cold sheets

beneath my words.

Your monsters

in my metaphors

and the silence of dying neurons

still cling

to life.


You let go too soon.

That's why you come back

through me.

But I'm only a poem.

Even with the big earrings

and the long dresses,

even as my words wear red

and wear the jewelry of your name,

I'm still only

a poem –

a poem of you,

a poem for you,

a new version

of Frida.

Your *Tree of Hope*

has deepened its roots.

My words grow

magnolia leaves

and your self-portraits;

they grow your *Flower of Life*

and your pet deer.

Everything you love

flourishes here,

things that, like you, died

before their time.

You make your colors bloom

next to mine,

and I dream your dream,

the last bloom of your tree.

You know the one.


Death

always sleeps

on the top bunk,

waiting

for the last leaf

to fall.

# *Thinking of You*

I write of death

and I think of you.

I think of you

and I write of death.

I know you both quite well.

You both possess

my sleepless nights

and my sleepless words,

rip the seams

of my metaphors,

the stitches of my scars

and yours.


I think of you

when I can't sleep.

I count skulls

and skeletons dressed in white,

a bowtie and a jacket.

I keep your memories

in my pocket.

Your paintings

are the kiss of death

on the skin of my face,

on the skin

of my poems.

So I write for you,

and about you

on a cool November night

in Houston, Texas,

when the moon feels full,

*"luna llena,"*

even though I know it's not.


Your full moons have come and gone

and they always return.

The skeletons we keep alive,

keep dressing and re-dressing,

the *naturaleza muerta*

we become.

## *Waves*

My moon is full tonight.

The tidal waves of my ocean

rise

and fall.

Thoughts crash and foam

against the shore

of my sanity.


I awaken from your dreams

wearing your past,

my own memories dressed as you.

How is it that you become me,

and why?


Is it that

we found each other

one lonesome night,

looking for a way to live...

looking

for a way to die?

Maybe we passed

each other by,

exchanging glances

from one life to the next.

We never rest.

We simply rise

and fall

like waves.

# *Llorona*

I.

*Dicen que soy alma vieja,*

*Llorona,*

*porque al nacer yo te vi.*

*Dicen que soy alma vieja,*

*Llorona,*

*porque al nacer yo te vi.*

*Que oscuro huipil llevabas,*

*Llorona,*

*que la Muerte te crei.*


*Que oscuro huipil llevabas,*

*Llorona,*

*que la Muerte te crei.*


*Ay de mi, Llorona, Llorona,*

*es que tus verdades me hablan.*

*Ay de mi, Llorona, Llorona,*

*es que tus verdades me hablan,*

*de amores de hoy y siempre,*

*Llorona.*

*Los que consumen el alma*

*de amores de hoy y siempre, Llorona,*

*los que consumen el alma.*

*Es que hay amores que viven,*
*Llorona,*
*hasta despues de la muerte.*
*En las paredes del tiempo esta escrito*
*que yo volveré a quererte.*
*En las paredes del tiempo esta escrito*
*que yo*
*volveré a quererte.*

*Ay de mi, Llorona, Llorona!*
*Llorona, sal ya del río.*

Ay de mi, Llorona, Llorona!

Llorona, sal ya del río.


Bien sabes que por las noches, Llorona,

el corazón siente frío.

Bien sabes que por las noches, Llorona.

El corazón siente frío.


Ay de mi, Llorona, Llorona.

Llorona,

de un Templo Santo.

Ay de mi, Llorona, Llorona.

No se,

como no amar tanto.

Ay de mi, Llorona, Llorona.

*No se,*

*como no amar tanto.*

*Cuando me lleves contigo, Llorona,*

*cobijame con tu manto.*

*Cuando me lleves contigo, Llorona,*

*cobijame con tu manto.*

II.

My words twist and turn

in pain.

How well they know

your name

and the whispers of your body,

the way your wounds

become art,

and how mine become poetry.

My broken heart

and my broken body

are always so intimate

with you.


And I am you again

tonight.

A shot of tequila

and the name of a man

between my breasts,

a longing

that never rests,

even if we were

to incinerate

the skeletons of the past –

the ones we keep

in the closet,

as if they could come to life.

Can they?

Can I?

Can I come back to life

like you do?


And who better than you

to understand

the pain and the scars

of loving this way,

giving ourselves completely

in every love

and in every secret.

That's how you grew

Magnolias

between your hands

and I grow words

that wear your dresses.


(Dress my skeletons.  Please.

Dress my skeletons.

Don't let them

go to bed cold.

Don't let them sleep alone

without feeling loved,

without feeling

remembered.)


That's what your paintings said

when you painted Death,

or fruit split in half

by the sword of silence,

the deafening silence

that made you paint *Diego*

in the center of your third eye...

Silence

that makes me write poems –

poems of eternal love,

poems

of eternal hunger.

Because we all know hunger.

Don't we?

All of us women know hunger,

hunger that makes us feed others,

forgetting about ourselves,

holding love

like you hold *Diego*

in your paintings,

like I nurse lovers

in my poems.

Woman's soul running on empty,

living

on passion alone

in a body that betrayed us

long, long ago.

Maybe that's why, year after year,

I find myself here

in this very moment of you:

*mis palabras vestidas de azul*

(my words dressed in blue) –

the blue of your sadness,

the blues

of your pain,

pain that becomes my own,

memories

carefully sewn

to the sheet

embracing my feet

when the monsters become real.

That's when our skeletons wear pink

and drink alone and sing

*con la voz de la Llorona,*

while exuding an aroma

of life

in the midst of death

and love

in the midst of sadness,

the legacy of you

and the madness

of your passions.


*Frida! Eternamente, Frida!*

*Hoy,*

*y por toda la vida,*

I shall

be

you!

## Silence

Memories shiver at times

when I think of you.

You take me back to the silence

of falling hair,

the coldness of scissors

against our past.

You and I alone at last...

alone

with our insanity.

I was six years old

when I leaned over the headboard

of my mother's bed

and cut my hair short.

There was something magical

about falling hair.


It made me feel in control.

I was never meant to be a doll.

My hair was that part of me

that still felt mine.

Yet, I cut it off

and watched it fall.


For a month

I looked like a boy,

a little boy in leg braces

and skirts,

carefully ironed shirts

and sorrow already stitched

to my flesh.


I have been you since age six

blending your colors

in my mix,

rotating rosary beads

between my fingers,

sadness that lingers

to this day.

You and I

have come a long way.


We learned to be alone

with our thoughts

and our fears,

alone

with the masks and the tubes

and the coldness

of ice cubes

on our lips.

The soul of your art still lives

beneath my long scar.


My poems undress themselves

into your past,

into the nakedness of white rooms

and brooms

that never learned to fly.


Sometimes,

the silence of falling hair

was loud,

loud like the screams of girls

whose heads were shaved

against their will.

"Head lice," the nurses said

as they looked at me,

scissors and razor in hand.

There was no G.I. Jane back then,

but there was Frida.

Your colors and my words

could scratch, bite, and curse

the meanest nurse.

Thank God

we never had to.


My hair is sacred now.

I don't punish myself

or my body.

I no longer go there...

to the silence

of falling hair.

I just trim the ends

and color the gray.

The rest of you

can stay.


I really don't know

how not to be you.

## About the Author

Maria R. Palacios is a poet, author, spoken word performer, motivational speaker, social change advocate, disability rights activist, and workshop facilitator. Featured on numerous local radio shows and podcasts, nationally syndicated programs, and in many international publications, Maria's impact on the rights of children, women, people with disabilities, and the Hispanic community is as immeasurable as her artistry is undeniable.

Some of Maria's most cherished accomplishments and positions include her participation in efforts that led to the passage of the Americans with Disabilities Act of 1990, being inducted into the Hispanic Women in Leadership Hall of Fame in 1996 and receiving the Hispanic Excellence Award in 1997, being a member of the International Guild of Disabled Artists and Performers since 2009, exploring her personal connection to Frida Kahlo through live performances of her poetry at Houston's annual Frida Fest celebration for seven straight years, participating in the Gulf Coast Poetry Tour (2009), and creating a publishing company (Atahualpa Press) that has brought five of her titles to life as well as two by other artists with disabilities.

Of particular passion to Maria is Sins Invalid, a performance project of artists with disabilities. With this group she has performed since 2007, co-facilitated their Tongue Rhythm Multi-Disciplinary Poetry Workshop in 2008, and is featured in the 2013 documentary, *Sins Invalid: An Unashamed Claim to Beauty in the Face of Invisibility*. In the artistic world, Maria is known as "The Goddess on Wheels."

palaciosmaria66@gmail.com

Printed in the USA
CPSIA information can be obtained
at www.ICGtesting.com
LVHW041109050924
790111LV00005B/520

9 780972 648387